Lifting The Sky

Myra Schneider

Ward Wood Publishing
www.wardwoodpublishing.co.uk

Published by Ward Wood Publishing
6 The Drive
Golders Green
London NW11 9SR
www.wardwoodpublishing.co.uk

The right of Myra Schneider to be identified as author of this work has been asserted by her in accordance with the Copyright, Designs and Patent Act, 1988.
Copyright © 2018 Myra Schneider
ISBN: 978-1-908742-68-1

British Library Cataloguing in Publication Data. A CIP record for this book can be obtained from the British Library.

Designed and typeset in Palatino Linotype
by Ward Wood Publishing

Cover artwork and design:
by Martin Parker at silbercow.co.uk © Martin Parker 2018

Printed and bound in Great Britain by
Imprint Digital, Seychelles Farm,
Upton Pyne, Exeter, Devon EX5 5HY

Contents

Part One

Part Two

Part Three

Part One

Winterlight

Dusk is dissolving the garden when you see
a bird alight on a skinny branch of the dying
pear tree. Above, the moon is a claw –
a delicate stroke in a Chinese painting.
You watch the sky, its intense blueing and blueing
which carries such a certainty of light
and you're tempted to believe it won't be folded
into the dark of night. Suddenly you're bending,
entering again that stone passage angled
to trap the midwinter sun and coddled
by stout walls which glow like softened gold.
At last, within the still chamber, you know
the innerness you've hankered for. Renewed,
you make your way to the dark world outside.

*The stone passage and inner chamber are references to Maeshowe
Neolithic tomb.*

7

The Stone

for Mimi

The moment of stepping from shade into a pool
of sun, of knowing I can still walk footloose,
lick the sea from my lips, climb cliff-high,

breathe in green on green: sycamore, beech,
hart's fern and a plant with ribbon leaves
I can't name though it's on the tip of my tongue –

becomes the moment I spot the emerald fist.
It's lodged in a stream among duller pebbles
and dotted with coral red, glints of amethyst.

This is an island full of fossils, rare rocks
and for minutes I'm on my knees, seven again,
dipping in water to my elbows, tugging the treasure

from its silt bed, drying it with tissues, stowing it
in a pocket of my flimsy sky-blue bag. Back
on the path, singing begins in my head.

Weeks later, pulling my prize from a drawer
I find it's now ash-grey, an awkward lump,
its brilliance dead – not a hint of jewel,

not even a trace of watercress or samphire green.
Examining the surface, I discover a few
faint magenta patches, a flattened face inlaid

with a line that worms into intimations of shells
and I come across tiny hillocks, holes –
wonder what gouged them, finger a shiny ridge.

So much history is here. I don't possess
the skill to unravel it from this welter of evidence.
But what holds me is the intense struggle

that the stone's twists and turns record. I read it
as the struggle to survive that's at the centre
of all being – and I love it for surviving.

Sutton Hoo

Meanings, which can't be unearthed by staring
at the intricate interlace of patterns in museums,
begin to emerge while we journey: the windings
of the Deben which carried the burial boat;
getting lost, a reminder that routes to the past
are not simple; trudging an unending field,
its soil ridged like the planks of a boat beneath
the leafy green crowns of potato plants.
At last, the mounds – not bumps, sharp hillocks
rising from grass the wind has paled and dried –
and more than I'd expected. I want to hold
their weightiness, breathe in their immense age.

And now, saddled with heat by a sullen sun,
twenty of us are climbing Mound One.
And even as I take a sip from a bottle
of warm water, even as I spot a girl
whose flaxen hair is ribboned with pink
and becomes a small me trowelling
for treasure, there's that nowness in the air
which phone addicts kill as they trample flowers
in parks, frighten away birds with beaks
full of twigs, ignore the trailing child
whose face is full of questions. Not one
of us crumples the nowness, its fine mesh.
Silent, we absorb this place where a king
was buried centuries ago with garnets
red as blood, with gold commanding as the sun.

*

Imagine day upon day digging
a trench deep into this mound, the labour
of shifting hundredweights of soil, imagine
the turning up of a piece of rusted iron.

Imagine the moment when Basil Brown
examines it, recognizes what it is:
a ship's rivet. Imagine the uncovering
of five nails red with corrosion,
the impression of a hull slowly emerging
in sand, its neatly overlapping planks
and the progress through the boat from rib to rib
until the mould from prow to stern is perfect.

We all see this and the man whose camera
dangles above his pudding belly, stops
taking photos. We gaze at prints of rowlocks,
patches marking the lie of rivets and a boat
as long as a pair of semi-detached houses,
long enough to seat forty rowers.
And now words I read decades ago,
by a poet whose name is lost, rise in my head:
his dread of high waves, his hard nights watching
from the prow in bitter winter, the huge water
almost freezing, icicles hung around him.
Yet he couldn't rest on land, spoke of *min hyge…*
mereflode… hwaelweg…gielleð anfloga –
his heart being with the sea, the whale's way,
his longing for the screams of the lone flyer.

Imagine that moment on the third of July
when Basil Brown poked an iron cauldron
and knew a burial chamber was probably
intact amidships, a chamber cradling
the bones of a man of high rank and the goods
he'd need as he sailed alone to the other world.

*

Is it because I am standing in this place
where a team of experts shovelled and sifted,
because I'm breathing the same grassy warmth
that I've become one of them, heaving

11

layers of blackened sand, lifting layers
of compressed decaying wood? I hear
someone mutter: *my godfathers*, turn to see
a small pyramid of gold and garnet.

Expectation rises with the temperature.
On many mornings heavy rain brings us
to a halt – not today. The sun's punishing
our heads as a purplish heap of metal is raised
and laid on the grass. A click – it's sprung open.
In the mustiness: a nest of silver bowls,
untouched, pristine, catching rays of light.

And now (which *now* is this?) treasures leap
from their museum cages: a gold buckle,
alive with the raised snouts and beaks
and claws of creatures, all of them looped
into patterns. Here's the plaque of a purse
with crimson wolves standing on hind legs,
their predatory mouths open. And look,
treasure which doesn't glitter: a rusted sword,
pieces of a helmet, the snake that rimmed its crown,
also knives, fragments of a lyre and scraps
specked with colour which turn out to be
a cap trimmed with otter fur, a cloak…

It seems there's no end to the buried marvels.
We've even begun to identify signs of life:
a crushed flower, a ladybird, traces of meat
on a dish, food to sustain the great king
on his journey, and beeswax in a holder –
a candle to lighten his heavy darkness.
We expect to dig up remains of his body,
haven't learnt that acid in the sand
is strong enough, over time, to dissolve
bone. Confounded, we go on searching
but find no vertebrae, no jut of shoulder blade,

no knuckle bones in skeletal fingers
not a knobble of ankle or knee. Strange
to find a wealth of grave goods, the print
of boat ribs but no hint of human ribcage.

Raedwold is nothing, nothing as those who buried
the boat, nothing as my parents on this day
at the end of May, my parents who had two
small children in nineteen-thirty-nine
but now have neither grave nor inscription,
who only exist in photographs, a boy
stiff as his boots, a little girl staring from
a locket, an old couple smiling in colour.

But they persist in a barometer, a desk,
the grief in a pot of buttons and safety pins,
in folders labelled *On His Majesty's Service*.
We think possessions are puppets hanging limp
on hooks unless we're present to flesh them out
but desk, purse and musical instrument
speak staunchly of us when we're dead.

*

Now, in the grassy swelter, we all forget
how we long for the lick of shade as the guide
re-creates the warrior king, a pagan
who decides to pay lip service to Christianity,
judges it diplomatic for life in this world,
and possibly the next, to plant a foot
in both camps. I glimpse him at Rendelsham
tipping mead and munching a haunch of meat
while heat roars from the fire and dyed hides
hold the winter-chill in the walls at bay.

And now I turn over and over scraps
about my grandmother who grew up
in a village like Chagall's somewhere near

Vitebsk, rose at dawn as a girl to take
the family's cow to pasture, later worked
in a shop, then followed her husband to London,
their one-up and one-down in Nelson Street,
east of Spitalfields, and how, after his death
she kept herself and her two sons by selling
bed linens on tick to other Jews.

And though I've walked Nelson Street, found
a few empty terraced houses as small
as the one she shared with another family
and a lodger, though the lead stove I saw
through a window made me cry, I know
how pale these resurrections are. We can't haul
the past up like a bucket of water from a well.
Kings and peasants, poets, mothers and fathers,
relatives who are only nameless faces
in photographs – they've all disappeared.

*

It's dusk now and I'm on the river path
from Woodbridge crossing water meadows. I peer
at the hill opposite but the mounds are hidden
by trees. The great air is sown with silence
and the milkiness from cooling grass is rising.
The smell drifts into the dimming light.
Strange darknesses beyond the reed beds
become a group of cows feeding intently
as I draw closer. When at last I turn
back towards the town, mist is laying
its whiteness over the low fields. The church
is almost smudged out and this century
with its cackle of rooves, masts and aerials
has gone. My small self dissolves in landscape.
The faint shape of a boat crossing the river.
Above the water, the thin cry of a bird.

A Nowhere Place

To sit on a cane chair by a pond that was once
a coach wash, a pond slicked with emerald scum
and so ticking with life it challenges death;

to sit under an umbrella sipping leaf tea, the sun
licking my face as if I was its lamb, is to unloosen
from my own, the world's distress and allow tears

to well. I tell myself I want nothing but to stay
in this spot by English willows reflecting
on the leafy stems they're dipping in water,

nothing but the china teapot, the strainer,
earl grey in the cup, green warmth cosseting my skin,
this silence surrounding pockets of sound.

It's not true. Already I'm seeking behind the inn sign,
beyond the croquet-hooped lawn, following a path
by a paddock where a solitary chestnut horse

hurries for the handful of stalks in the flat
of my hand. I wonder if the animal wants
connection with another creature as much as hay.

The mute tension of rabbits. By the nettle-lavish hedge
two are crouched on haunches, long ears raised
for messages far beyond my range of hearing. And now

I know what I want is to lie down in this nowhere
that's borne so much, breathe in its earthiness,
absorb its pulse, believe in its continuance.

The Composition Hut

Fairytale: the fierce slope of the roof, the pines,
the lake, so it's easy to fold up this century,
its quick screens, its cables packed under streets.
Now is this green and blue silence, the hut
at the foot of the hill where Grieg worked.
I can almost see his newly-hatched shoals
of crochets and quavers. So why am I holding back?
The door's unlocked – once inside wouldn't my ideas
flow? No, I'd be beguiled by the spears of light
rising from the silkgrey water, by the voice urging
the rowers in that boat and I'd float to yesterday
when I saw a lifetime of waterfalls, mountains clad
with firs all pointing at ever. Lulled, I'd believe
the future safe, let littlefish words evade my fingers…

Months on, the composition hut is still in my head.
It's a hermitage where I could uncover layers of self
but does self have any meaning on its own?
I have no answer, only know I need the pines,
the lake of serenity, the idea of the hut as a retreat
or a perching place, at least, for my soul
where I can begin to face the discomposure
of composing and, undistracted, follow the thoughts
slippery as eels travelling beneath the surface,
let them lead me to the disruption and pain
beyond the trees. For when I shut off the outer tick
I find myself listening to the quickening beat
of this dear planet as if it were my own heart's clock.

Grieg's Composition Hut at Troldhaugen.

Dunwich

J M W Turner, Dunwich, c.1830

The higgle of pale houses, the church
perched on the clifftop and the gleam, eerie
as a cat's eye, in the tower's upper window

draw me in. The village already seems
to be no more than a ghost. Below it
two cliff shoulders curve inland

like those of a resigned beast pulling
a heavy load in a farmer's cart.
Mute, they withstand the ocean's

white lashings which look certain to continue
for hours. Beyond the tousled shore
men are struggling with a wooden boat.

My heart sinks when I discover they are trying
to launch it in the fuming waters, not land it.
Then I realize the specks on the turf slopes

are people gathering to watch. Peering,
I make out a fleck on the horizon, am sure
it's the sail of a fishing boat in distress

and in my head I hear that hymn of long ago
at school: *for those in peril on the sea...*
Today I'm standing on these now lopped cliffs

in August sun – not a trace of church,
the only dwellings ex-coastguard cottages.
I gaze at gorse, at ants massing on sand,

at the ocean docile as a sleeping dog,
utterly unlike the savage creature
Turner saw. But how long before

even this subdued hill and its crumble-paths
to the sea are toppled in a storm,
dragged away by waves, devoured?

Windows
for John

Today November's in deep despond. From indoors
I watch it creeping up from the stream at the foot of the park
like a stray mongrel trailing thin breath over the grass.

All day the grey, low-bellied sky weighs me down. I pine
for a hint of tangerine, of rowan-berry but hopelessness,
like the damp, is quick to nose its way into everything.

I smell it in the drawer by the kitchen sink, smell it
as I squelch through muddied leaves in the copse, stare
at it when I reach the tree felled by last month's storm,

feel it in the shock of its wrenched-out roots. The split trunk
gaping is a reminder of the loop of islands whose towns
and villages were helpless when a typhoon swept through.

All afternoon night threatens to snuff the failing light
but at dusk the sky quietly cracks. Strands of eggshell-blue
with white streamers spread, cranberry pools emerge.

Then the moment I open the front door, stand spellbound:
on the other side of our nondescript road the upper
      windows
of a semi are transformed to sheets of a luminous scarlet

so dazzling it's as if the panes are generating sunset. If only
it was possible, before darkness swallows the last of day,
to funnel off this incandescence and keep it for our future.

Returning

Once again May has grabbed me by the scruff,
again I've sloughed off the winter sleep
of forgetting, am stunned by new green dotting
trees, how it unfolds in leaps and bounds
on verges, in rail sidings, depot yards
and every handkerchief of waste ground.
It's as if I've never looked at the freckles
of milky florets cramming hawthorn twigs,
the clots of elderflowers. And although once
I was wild as fieldside brambles it's as if
I've never fingered newly risen grasses:
feather-headed fescue, the whiskers of barley
or the brush heads of timothy, have just learnt
that warmth makes a bed in untamed grass
which covets clover and white parsley umbrellas.
I breathe in the sweet extravagance,
dream I'll come back as grass or blossom
until a voice in my head mocks with lists
of droughts, names of extinct species. I think
of vanished sparrows and how often the stream
in the park is dry-lipped, the earth pocked
with cracks. And it yawns before me: the possibility
of fescue, flowers, leaves not returning.

Seahorses

They look unfishlike and so unlikely, upright
in the water, could easily be taken for cousins
of stick horses with their tapering tails,
ribbed spines and equine-shaped snouts.

No surprise they swim poorly but the internet
reveals they're full of surprises: the bones
circling their heads to form coronets,
their courtship that begins with partners bowing

to one another, a prelude to linking tails
and waltzing serenely as a couple in the glitter
of a stately ballroom, then hours later
rising in spirals from the seabed. I smile

as I watch a pair in a video that's so fairytale
I wonder if they'll metamorphose into a prince
and princess but the facts of their unexpected story
outdo fantasy. A real gentleman, the male

receives his mate's eggs in his mouth – yes, it's he
who takes on the pregnancy and how touching
that his sweetheart visits him each morning.
Their lives, meandering edges of the sea

and anchoring themselves to its trailing fronds,
seem idyllic so I don't want to discover
that seahorses are over-fished, often end
up as dinner delicacies and Chinese remedies,

don't wish to know they're likely to disappear.
I want to daydream, as I luxuriate in shallows
among shells and underwater grasses,
I'm in a world where it's safe to forget fear.

Daggers of Light

stabbing and stabbing – the rest is blank.
A wound somewhere, pain's knifing into
a knee. Blurred islands, violet as bruises,
swell behind eyes.
                              I've no idea what I am.
Sand is bedding back and shoulders, damp
slime-green hairs have entangled fingers,
waves are lapping on a shore.
                              Is this death then?
The heap of wooden ribs over there might be
the carcase of a boat with its snout jutting
or the skeleton of an animal the sea's washed in.
The stone by my hand is a worry – so ominous,
the black hole screwdrivered into its face.
                                        But look,
the sand's stamped with shells – here's one
that's pearl-silver and flat as a button.
Perhaps I've tumbled on a patch of paradise,
its rock pools and limpets?
                              This tuft of pink
is sea-thrift and up there above the shingle –
yes, it's a clump of samphire. It reminds me
of the old man with empty eyes and the tramp
who told him he'd fallen from a cliff top
but by a miracle survived.
                              A tangle of weeds
fleshy as a placenta covers my feet.
It all fits now – I'm still alive but what is lost,
oh what is lost, what can never be retrieved,
is my dear friend.
                              I must gather up her words:
this gannet… whole being flowing forward…
stow them in my bag, scramble up the unkind
shingle shelves, set off again on the road.

for Mary MacRae

The Thing

The windows are listless and the worn-down steps
to the pavement remind you of cracked lips.
The mean road mutters it has no ending.

Above, pouting sky and a chill in the air,
omens of imminent rain. No cat sitting
watchful on a wall, no sign of anything alive,

not even the worming of a dandelion stem.
Oh for buttercup curtains instead of the silent
shoulder to shoulder hostility of these houses.

Have the inhabitants fled? A door wedged open
with a mat. If you push inside you'll only be greeted
by long-abandoned clothes and the stench of decay.

Listen, there seems to be a choir chanting
at the end of the hall passage. It tugs you past
uncertain banisters and into a room dense

with a residue of soot and damp. Here's the settee
and tiled mantelpiece of your childhood, the grate
heaped with ash. Is this death? The sound

changes to the yammering of a newly-born creature.
It jabs and jabs at your head. You long to fly
from the demand but it's impossible. Kneeling down,

you make out, in the dim of the fireplace, a minute
shapeless thing, a mess of mucous and blood
plastering skin roughed with what might be

the first sproutings of feathers. Its helplessness
is total, its desperation to be alive ruthless.
What can you offer? Gingerly you pick it up.

Reflections

1

Beyond the windows: an enticing word lit
by buds on turquoise branches of candelabras.

It offers waiters, sleek black-and-white birds,
hurrying laden plates to tablecloths

alive with cutlery, dazzle spots in bottles
and glasses half-filled with ruby wine,

There are many faces. That one whose eyes
are searching, searching – might it be yours?

2

Quick, quick you pass through two sets
of swing doors eager to immerse yourself

in the luminosity, stumble upon
disappointment. Faces, tablecloths, colours

have all dissolved and the building behind you
has disappeared. In this dim wilderness

it's hard to believe anything exists.
Even you might be a figment of imagination.

3

Lost, you inch forwards in the hope of finding
a way out of such a desolate place,

search for a gatepost, a pathway, any speck
that shows signs of life, listen in vain

for footsteps, clothes rustling, wings flapping.
At last it seems you are making your way down

a church aisle of trees towards quiverings
on what might be a strip of water.

4

You pick your way to a pool that's little more
than a measly puddle. The ground around it

is stony and thistles prickle your legs
as you peer beneath quavering silver slivers.

There's nothing but water opaque as rock,
as the density of despair. In vain you search

for the source of the worming light flickering
on the surface. It must be an illusion.

5

You hate the pool for its deception
but can't tear yourself away. Suddenly,

far down at a depth you'd no idea could exist
in such shallowness, you see a coin of moon

purposeful as hope. Next to it is a face,
not a narcissistic face only capable

of adoring itself, a naked face, yours.
It's willing now to see itself, accept the truth.

This sequence was inspired by the work of Robert Aldous.

The Tubular Bells

were a surprise. At first I thought
they were icicles in a frozen waterfall
but they seemed to be fluid as honey

dropping from a comb. Then I noticed
the kitchen table and washing machine
were edgeless, melting away

and I wondered if they'd been magicked
by the instrument, its gold that was so unlike
the sleekness of a Pharaoh's death mask,

the solidity of Cellini's over-elaborate
salt cellar or the jewel-studded crown
worn by Holy Roman Emperors –

such symbols of pomp, self-importance.
The bells summoned buttercups, lilies,
their stamens tipped with orange powder,

the different ochres of fallen leaves
For moments I believed they were healing
the wounded world but they disappeared.

Hopeless, I stood by the January window
until I saw dusk was rivering the sky
with saffron and lemon, took heart.

The Pear Tree

It arose with an intensity I can't put into words
as I fumbled through wilderness, not as it is now –
bony-elbowed, shrunk, half its remaining limbs
useless and smothered in lichen and moss – no,

it was in its prime, branches worshipping the sky's blue,
twigs exuberant, not caring a damn that nothing lasts,
that April, the cruellest month began tomorrow.
And I was dizzy with happiness to see the tree massed

with blossom, the stamens in each floret erect, eager
for pollination. The air was so pungent with fecundity
I reached up, found hard green swellings
and at once a white multitude of petals fluttered away.

In moments the months skipped, grizzled and blustered
through summer and I was bathed in the apricot light
of September. The birds and I were now competing
for the tree's treasure, wasps were mobbing fruits

oozing on the grass. Sweet flesh was on my tongue
when the woodcutter butted in and I was perplexed
to see he was the double of our easygoing gardener.
The branches stiffened as he raised his axe.

Terrified, I stood against the trunk, arms spread.
My eyes opened to a fogbound winter morning.
Stumbling to the window, I saw the old tree ethereal,
clothed in frost. Above it a pale sun was emerging.

The First of Spring

for Anne Cluysenaar

A honey sun, the cease of gnawing wind
so we seize the day, unleash ourselves
in the country park, gaze at flowers inscribed *To Dad*

lying on a bench. They summon a huge bee
to their pink and yellow freesia bells. Dreamily,
I too enter the nectar-laden chambers and feed.

Turning away, we follow *the droghte of March* track
to the water garden where snowdrops are fading,
daffodils are on the brink of opening

and expectation's in bloom on naked trees.
Welters of lily stalks in the darks of a pond
are tangles of umbilical cords. Beyond the garden,

beyond the singing of birds is a lake which glitters
as if it's a source of light. We sit down
on a wicker seat and there you are breathing

in the budding warmth, freed from the last
of October now and that distressed message
you sent before your life was snatched.

You're stooping over a small plant, stroking
its leaves, tracking the hover-rise of a damsel-fly,
smiling as you follow all the riverlets.

Part Two

Discovering Medusa

The head had haunted him ever since the day
he'd rashly promised his mother's devious lover:
'I will bring you whatever gift you wish.' Sometimes

he dreamt the Gorgon eyes were turning him
to stone and he was trying to choke out cries
for help. Sometimes he believed the hideous woman

was stalking him in a passageway or crouched
like a ravenous lion waiting to spring out
from behind a column or an olive tree's twists.

But now as he neared her lair on a desolate shore
where the sea was ominously still, the air
weighty with silence, the only sign of life

a gull circling the sky, the time had come
to discard fear like a tunic, forget the beaches
where he wrestled with friends, swam with dolphins

or lazed in the sapphire-blue, be grateful for a helmet
which made him invisible, take danger
by the horns. Beyond a jagged arch in the rocks,

near a stretch of seaweed-smothered stones,
he saw a cleft in the cliffs. His body bristled
as if to defend itself but he raised his sword

and positioned the mirror shield so that it kept
the cave in sight as he crept towards its stink
of rotting oyster shells and fish bones.

She emerged clumsily, clad in a tattered gown
and sniffing as if suspicious of a presence.
Without flinching he looked at the snakes tangling

on her head, her eyes red as an enraged bull's,
the bulging cheeks and the open distorted mouth
which suddenly let out a series of shrieks.

Swift as a swallow he dived behind her, summoned
all his strength and with a single blow severed
the head from the neck, then reeled backwards,

didn't see the white-winged horse springing
into the air from her spilt blood. Shuddering,
he shut the head, eyes still glaring, in a box.

In spite of success he was troubled by a sense
of wrong he couldn't identify. He charged down
to the sea and waded in, welcoming its salt sting,

swam till he was cleansed. Then feeling free
of the monstrous woman, he lay on the sand, let
the sun lick his skin. Aware of a shadow,

he looked up, saw a sylph-like girl robed
in saffron. Her delicacy took his breath away.
'I want to unfold the truth to you, Perseus.'

Her voice was soft as feathers, clear as a flute.
What trick was this? He tensed as if struck
by a stone. Although he'd no idea who she was

she seemed familiar. Coldness ran through him
but he felt impelled to follow her to a temple.
When they entered it a wave with a snowy crest

which had trapped the sun's dazzling rays, swept
through the building. The water vanished quickly
and before them stood Poseidon, half-naked.

Face greedy, he grabbed hold of the maiden,
flung her to the floor in front of Athena's statue
and tore off her gown although she struggled

like a terrified deer. Perseus tried to plunge
at the god, pinion his arms but he was rooted
to the spot and it seemed a voice whispered to him:

'A spell forced me to comply.' Desperate, he beat
at the empty air but it was solid as a wall
and soon his knuckles were bruised and bleeding.

A zig-zag of lightning and Athena appeared.
He gasped. Poseidon had disappeared. The goddess
accused: 'Woman, you've desecrated my temple.'

She raised her hand. Shocked, Perseus watched
the girl's beauty draining like wine from a cup,
her youthful face yellowing, her mouth hardening,

her hair thickening and twisting into snakes.
He shouted but the two figures and the temple
had dissolved and he was lying on the empty beach,

the midday sun burning his face. Despair
tumbled upon him like a boulder from a mountain.
Why had Athena punished a raped maiden,

why ensured he would murder her by arming him
with a mirroring shield? What did living mean
if he was no more than a puppet of the gods?

The sea was hissing: *abuse, abuse* as if
it was spreading news of the sea god's act
far and wide to plant evil in minds.

Better to end his own shameful misery
by throwing himself into the ocean, better
to let a shark feast on his body than endure

years struggling with the gnawing pain of guilt.
'No, you were my saviour, freed me from torment
with a skilful blow, live and thrive.' The voice

was beside him but thin as gossamer. He wept.
The easy life he'd led for twenty years belonged
to another world. Sombrely, he gathered up

the sword, the shield, the terrible gift, re-traced
his steps through the arch in the cliff. Until the day
he died gentle Medusa would be his head.

Blue

Once again you've been catapulted into it.
The steel-blue shock goes deeper than you thought possible,
is maybe bottomless. The problem is how to stay afloat
on these waters – their weight would be unbearable.

You know now blue is cold anger and more dangerous
than red's leaps of rage. The anger isn't yours – it's the fury,
implacable as a brick wall, which you never try to confront
because you're certain it will drown you.

This time, trapped in a fragile boat, breath battering
your chest, you're spun round and round, a plaything
to be swept into Machiavellian currents, raised for seconds
by everests of spume-capped waves, then plunged

into gullies which shift. In desperation you pull
on the oars but you're propelled past cliffs whose sickly shine
in the ferocious midday sun makes you dizzy
and you're terrified the end will be death by water.

Time has gone overboard. Is it days or years
that you've been floundering? Somehow you grit yourself
to face the fuming swirl head on and although buffeted,
you steer at last into a quiet passage, reach port.

The fear clamping mind and body falls off
but the solid ground you ached for rocks beneath your feet
and though you grasp the fabric of your life, determined
to preserve every thread of it, blue's still lapping at your heels.

Anne Askew

For refusing to be muzzled by her husband
as other wives were and striking out on her own path,
for her quick educated mind, her ability to discourse with learned men,
I shall remember her.

For her resolve to go to London, seek out thinkers
and interpret the bible, risky even though the king by taking
the title Supreme Head of the Church, had opened the door to enquiry,
I shall remember her.

For her passionate preaching of the gospels,
not being cowed when arrested and thrown into prison
but refuting the persecutors who tried to force-feed her Catholic beliefs,
I shall remember her.

For her canny evasions and logical arguments,
for answering tartly when the stricture was hurled: 'A woman
has no more business with the scriptures than a sow has wearing a saddle,'
I shall remember her.

For expounding metaphors in the Bible:
'We are not to take Christ as the material thing by which
he's signified for then we would make him a door, a lamb, a vine, a stone…'
I shall remember her.

For the fire, not the fire built up at Smithfield
but that fire in the belly that gave her the strength to endure
the rack which wrenched her shoulders and hips out of their sockets,
I shall remember her.

For the fire which inspired her poems
and writings about her trials, the fire which made her hold fast
as the awed crowd gasped and unstoppable flames snatched at her flesh,
I shall remember her.

Anne Askew: 1521-1546. The 1534 Act of Supremacy granted Henry VIII Royal
Supremacy which meant he was declared the supreme head of the church in England.

Nameless

Hours later, when she's unspooled her story
eight times and a scream's gathering inside her,
the detective inspector lets her go. She glances
at a clump of policemen conferring in a van
outside the park, at the wrought iron gates
erected by a long-forgotten peer, now looped
with chains and guarded by a young constable
who's fending off questions. Then she trudges
past gardens with mock urns, pointless daffodils.
The dog, longing to be free, drags on his lead.

Later, still shaken, Elena sits in the kitchen
drinking tea and tells herself it was obvious
the detective hadn't discovered a single thing
about who the woman was or how she'd died.
She replays the dog's mounting distress,
the clambering through bushes to banks pale
as toothless gums, the shock of unzipped anorak,
pallid skin, muddied blouse, its pearl buttons.
The woman was little more than a slip of a girl,
thirty at most – somebody's daughter.

She dials her own daughter in Inverness,
is irritated by the sighed: 'Mum, you've just retired
from years of teaching, you're not responsible
for bodies in streams,' the snapped 'for God's sake!'
when she hints against taking off alone
in the wilds. Wishing she'd rung a friend instead,
she puts the radio on but it doesn't silence
voices in her head debating if the woman, depressed
by splitting with her partner, had drunk too much
in *The Swan*, tottered down to the stream and slipped.
Nor does it blot an image of hands at her neck.

After five days the gates are unlocked.
On edge, Elena watches runners practising
for marathons, pram-pushers, terriers sniffing
at stalks and lunch-time kids dropping chips –
all indifferent to the dead girl. She avoids
the bend in the stream near the playground,
pours scorn on herself for peering at darknesses
between trees, roars at the dog for scaring
a moorhen from its throne of twigs, exchanges
meaningless words with familiar faces.

Daily, she expects news from the police. None.
A request from school, to come and help children
struggling with English, throws her into a dither.
Lilac's in bloom when a paragraph in the paper
with the headline *Murder?* tells her the woman –
not named as if to erase her identity –
had been missing for a month. She pauses
by the ranks of hedge parsley on the river's
unmown banks, struck by nature's ability
to shrug off death, concentrate on continuance,
wants to lose herself in the lacy white layers,

to forget the shrunken waters and lifeless face.
But she shoves away the desire to escape,
walks on. The cheerful dog, as if applauding,
scrambles out of the dirty stream showering
liquid diamonds, drops a ball he's rescued
at her feet, waits. She throws it as far as she can
and as though a misted glass has suddenly cleared
she sees how she longs to return to teaching.
At the bend by the playground she stoops and picks
some buttercups for remembrance, drops them
in the water, watches the petals float away.

Survival

1

When the cot wouldn't stop howling
night unstitched its gentle blanket and smacked

the kitchen clock's face. Death was a vision
of a bloated sheep slowly floating downriver.

By day I was trapped in the tube of the hoover's
extended arm, fear filled my lungs with dust.

The years ahead stood before me blank
as a line of empty buckets but I knew they'd fill

with panic, its manic dance as time and again
I failed to measure up as a real mother.

2

When I received the diagnosis death jumped up
taller than life, laughed at the bright words

the consultant was mouthing and pointed its gun
at my head. Reeling, I looked into its two nostrils.

The words crumpled. Then the walls collapsed
as if they were the pieces of paper the wolf

had huffed. We drove home and the future
fled along the gutters with the thunder-rain,

so hurling my favourite teacup – the one patterned
with redcurrants across the kitchen – was useless.

And yet somewhere inside the empty self
were threads I didn't know I possessed.

Love was it? kindness? that tugged, set me
on my feet, worked my arms and legs.

There was the day when a girl in mauve
put a tray of powder paints into my hand

and I unleashed on sugar-paper treefuls
of turquoise leaves, a pram with easy wheels.

There was the day, years on, when snowdrops,
defying the forest of bare twigs above them,

stopped me in the street, spurred me to latch
onto words, defeat the terror lodged in my head.

3 AM

I'm moonless as tonight's sky, helpless
as a rabbit's blind and furless kits
and in my body's cave misgivings hang
from the walls like folded wings. To combat

thumping pain and racing fear, I picture
a Matisse-red room with French windows,
potted palms and a half-naked woman
lounging on a sofa, then the yellow surprise

of the first drifts of daffodils trumpeting
spring to morose February this morning.
It doesn't work and the silence is implacable
as the dark – I wish it purred like the cat settling

her warm self into the curve of my spine
to sleep but the black cat has long gone.
A tremble in the air – and there are my friends,
shadowy at first beyond my bed. Their outlines

slowly fill out with muted colours and now
they're facing each other in two rows
as if for a formal dance. They reach out,
join hands across the divide. I gaze

at their arms which seem to form the ribs
of a boat, the kind ancient kings were buried in
but this is no death ship – it's a hammock
they've created for me. The moment I lie down

it takes my body's burden. No one speaks
but touch has its own language. I let go
of distress and feel such lightness of being
I could lift off into the blue like a damselfly.

Losing
for Stephen

Every sock in the bunch you're holding
is a dangling single. You wonder how many more
must be mouldering, partnerless, stuck in drawers.

Later, on the way to work, you remember
the lost mug patterned with rosemary you think
an absent-minded friend slipped into her bag,

and picture the half-dead umbrella you left on a bus.
But all this is trivial on a day when the smudged air
is buzzing with the loss of jobs, self-respect, children.

Hopeless, you fold the newspaper, turn to now –
this moment on a train underground: that black lad,
beautiful in his pale blue anorak. You try to work out

why his hands are shading his eyes. To block out
the world as he listens to the sounds wires
are bringing to his ears? To survey the carriage?

Already this now has passed out of reach, become
a memory which will sink or swim among millions
of others in your mind's measureless caverns.

And now, you visualize time as unstoppable sand falling
through a sieve, count the growing refusals
of your body. They remind you a moment will come

when you'll lose the privilege of consciousness,
remind you not to hang around limply as a sock
but to forestall this last loss with findings:

a sparrowhawk perched on your gate, eyes alert
for prey, words that toadleap from imagination,
from heart – to make sure every day is a finding.

Le Cheval

after Matisse

I'm in the pink, a pink that revels
in rose, magenta, cerise, that ripples
with prance and dance. Muzzle down,

ears pricked, I'm chomping to run over
milky grass, leap fences and streams
with the air rushing past my flanks.

Swiftness is the be and end all
but difficult for him – the old man
whose scissored child I am.

Mostly he's tethered to chair or bed.
I am his running. While he dreams me
he's young again, a frolicking colt.

Look how he proclaims my emergence
in a Mediterranean of blue, look
I'm poised to canter over curving green!

The little islands floating around me,
are they leaves or birds? Who can guess
what this long worming of yellow is?

Who cares! I'm fizzing so don't snort:
dreams are figments. I'm here in the pink,
you're staring at me open-mouthed!

Insanity

The air's unstiffened – today it smells of sun,
of the green that feeds grass and I feel a lifting
as if the weighty cloak of winter has fallen

from my shoulders. I wonder why that dog trotting
along the path is in a posh crimson coat
which is labelled *Barking Mad* and hiding

the creature's chestnut gloss? My eyes alight
on the buttoned-up owner – not a flicker
of humour on his face. In seconds I delete

the words stitched in a loud red and transfer
them to his back, walk on smiling. At home
politicians' insanities pepper our supper:

the *green* speeches they make while planes zoom
from new runways, the waving of democracy
as though it were a flag at an international game.

It doesn't help to picture them as orchestras
of Neros playing pretty tunes. Upstairs
I struggle with clots of words, try not to see

that long dachshund body with spaniel ears
trapped in clownish clothes. At ten I escape
to watch a TV film but it's set in a war.

The camera's panning over faces lost in sleep
when from next door a mighty hammering
makes our rows of books shudder and me leap

to my feet. Could somebody be raiding
the empty house stripped for re-wiring? Is a ghost
that's been trapped inside the boiler clamouring

for freedom? I make a phone call and at last
the builder turns up, searches from loft
to basement, finds nothing. In bed I can't rest,

listen for explosions, collapsing walls, then drift
round the house like a moth. The moon confounds
me with eerie silver lines between rifts

in clouds. I close my eyes, picture that hound
curled up, unaware of any state of mind.

It Was

the day a hinge detached itself,
making the wardrobe door keel over
without warning and lean
its weight against my weakling shoulder
while I yelled for help;

the day the telephone engineer
lay flat out on the floor, half his bum
on view, as he tried to identify
which cable was causing all the crackles
drowning conversations.

It was the day the weather
kept grizzling and the washing machine
went through its cycle of work as usual,
giving no hint it was weeping
buckets all over the kitchen floor,

the day my keys vanished
and although I searched the cutlery drawer,
the kitchen bin and even the oven,
they kept mum in the flowery folds
of an umbrella until the witching hour.

It was the day I mopped up
the washing machine's misery, dialled
a friend as soon as the reborn phone
offered glorious clarity,
and let my tongue run away with itself;

the day the three-legged
and tail-less cat, who's taken ownership
of our garden, made me gasp
at the speed she achieved
in chasing away a tabby invader;

the day the world praised the little town
of Modbury for banning plastic bags
because creatures on the Pacific's shores
were choking to death
on plastic scraps washed in by the sea.

It was the night I leant out
of my bedroom window to look at the clouds
folding up their heavy linen
and saw in the deep blue a thin moon
with a cow perched on each horn.

It's Sensitive

he says, *no need to press the buttons hard –*
stroke them. Sensitive to whom? I wonder
and Shelley's plant rises before my eyes.

He peers at me through severe lenses as if
suspecting I mistreat it so I don't say
its sensitivity seems to be an excuse

for shirking work, don't remark its forbears
willingly washed three towels at a time
but it rejects more than two as overload

and if pushed it donkey-plods, leaves
a dripping heap in its hub. And I don't complain
it roughs up jumpers in its whirring darkness.

Sensitive my foot, I mutter when I climb
into bed that night. In a dream I confront
the gleaming white, implacable body

and, scorning its beckoning dials, raise an axe
in a surge of hate, smash its smugness.
Behind it I see the long-gone machines,

hefty, unsophisticated, trusty
as sheepdogs. But next morning I find it
quite unblemished and white as innocence

belittling the kitchen sink. Sensitive!
The word clangs as I feed it socks and shirts.
Cursing, I stroke its buttons, catch it smirking.

Consider Your Shoulders

and how unkindly you treat them, forever
insisting they carry your unwieldly baggage.
Take today – you forced them to rise and mutate
to humps solid as granite all because
the driver of a van backed into your garden,
announced he'd come to deliver nine boxes
of vanilla rice dream, and when you told him
you'd only ordered one and were not the school
he'd expected, didn't have a trolley to wheel them away,
he retorted, face hardening, *you paid for the stuff.*
Then, instead of slamming the door when he began
to fetch them, you stood there speechless,
re-living the crates of milk from all those years ago
waiting in the school canteen, implacable
as punishment with their sickly white smell,
flimsy straws, liquid which lay heavy
as the classroom on your stomach. And you gawped
at the buttercup-yellow cartons clinging together,
not cows' milk but a rice nightmare which would weigh
on you long beyond the use-by date. Even
when the van vanished into the endless maze
of outer London and from checking through emails
on the machine your shoulders hate, you ascertained
you'd only been charged for a single box;
even when you smiled and felt triumph swell
like sound from the silver mouth of a lifted trombone,
your shoulders were too stressed to budge, as if
what lay beyond the front door wasn't roads
with grass verges, trees and complacent semis
but browbeaten streets riddled with danger.

Instructions

Today we shall all be water pipes,
   she said, pipes that know nothing of slouch
      but stand upright against walls to let water
         travel unimpeded into baths, basins, radiators.

Becoming pipes means unlocking
   shoulders, ironing out kinks in backs
      and knots in knees, challenging faulty hips,
         waking up feet, exulting in the glory of flow.

In our new roles we shall be carriers
   of water which blesses grass and flesh,
      water which has no crises of confidence,
         offers itself freely even though we mistreat it.

Now we have re-invented ourselves
   see how tall we are, tall as organ pipes,
      as telegraph poles. Everything is possible
         if we don't stifle, but let in imagination, its music.

Listen, the sound is as uninhibited
   as rain. Inexperience is unimportant –
      we shall practise the ocho step, enjoy
         the brush of thigh against thigh, enter the rhythm,

draw all the excitement in its emotion
   into our bodies, move with the clear intention
      of a young river. In reality, as well as fantasy,
         each one of us will become a dancer of the tango.

Ocho step: the basic 8-count in Argentine Tango.

Cold

a tidal wave sweeping over a floor
where rugs are small hopeless islands.
Cold subduing the four walls, sniggering
into my neck, making its breath mine.

To escape
I squeeze under the thin duvet
but the bed's implacable as a tombstone.
Damp right through, you'll catch your death,
my dead mother ominous as ever.
Shan't, I snap back, haul my jumper
over my nightdress, then bully socks
onto ice-block feet, pull on my beetroot hat,
curl up in foetal mode.

Eyes closed, I delete
the glacial stairs, the many-doored passage
that's never discovered the meaning of heat,
the farmer's wife: *you'll be cosy in bed,*
will myself downstairs to the redhot range
that's trumpeting sizzling chicken and potatoes
bursting from their thermal jackets.

Then, I conjure
bonfires' roaring hearts, scalding radiators,
the stuffy Underground, that sultry Tobago beach
where silky sand almost burns skin
from the soles of feet.

Into my warm fold
I urge orphan lambs lost on the moors,
Oliver Twist daring to hold out his bowl,
the woman I saw last year on Waterloo Bridge,
her bare feet blued by a whipping March wind,
those without homes or not at home in themselves
and unable to articulate their grief.

                              I awaken
to streaming light. Bleatings tug me to the window
to marvel at the many scatterings of sheep in fields
eiderdowned in white and glittered by sun.
Re-dressed, I run down to the kitchen purring heat.

Kitchen

Begin in the kitchen, its yellow cupboards always
hustling to be opened, its noticeboard
crammed with postcards and faded messages,
begin at suppertime by the open door
where the honey scent of buddleia is floating in
from the garden with the reassuring hum of trains,
begin with pouring milk over bowls of raspberries
which you grow to succour mind as well as body.
Begin with those ginger stains, reminders
that the table's painted white surface is a mistake.

But thoughts can't always be directed and today
the kitchen drifts back to the one above
the Clyde, a utility cloth on the enamel table,
my parents ruling from chairs at each end, the cat
dozing on the haybox, Sheila and I glued
to Daddy's story of Torquemada Blenkinsop
and crocodiles on the Amazon
                                                  till Mummy
spoils it clattering plates, and the wireless is tuned
to drone news about the war with the Germans,
news that will stop if the war is ever over,
news which makes Daddy purse his lips
and means battleships down on the Firth
and bombs falling in faraway London,
war that's useful for orphaning dolls upstairs
but is boring as the unending washing up
in the scullery, boring which Sheila and I escape
at night by flying our beds across the moors
to the woods dark as witches where magic happens.

In the fogged distance you say: 'It's the end
of the *News of the World*.' 'Good,' I mumble, staring
at the red liquid trickling down my fingers. It spots
the table which suddenly slips into your mother's –

the one we used for years until its legs
aged and wobbled –

           and there she is in her kitchen
at Stamford Hill, her smile through her glasses warm
as her cherry cheeks, her pinafore plumpness,
the smell of goulash and dumplings from the stove
as she welcomes me to the house which she bought
eighteen years after the Nazis snatched
her home in Inzersdorf. Excited, she shows me
the pottery she's made: a heart-shaped dish,
a plate with leaf shapes stamped on cobalt
and freckled olive, a generous jug.

                I try to imagine,
as I didn't decades ago, what it must mean
to be deprived of your home, leave your streets,
relatives, country, language and with two children
and just the possessions you can squeeze into
suitcases, travel fearfully by train and boat
to England, be thankful, trudge through years
of lowly work. Would you ever feel rooted again
whatever house you eventually own,
however fine the works of art you create?

Taking the damp cloth you're holding out,
I glance at the leafy plate that's now on our wall –
such confident leaves patterning its circle.
You start doing the washing up, I wipe
the spilt raspberry juice from the table.

How It Is

After weeks of gutters spewing rain, December
has flown in and a mist pale as goose down
is hovering over park and garden. The smell of frost,

the naked trees catapult me back to the girl
I once was, spellbound by Anglo-Saxon poems
in the rigid silence of the university library

on a thin winter day. Like that girl, who felt
she didn't belong, I hanker for the distant past
but cocooned in my home's humming warmth,

I forget heatless rooms hoard a chill which seeps
into flesh, forget cold's a beast which can bite
so deeply it stops breath and snuffs the mind

lodged in the body's cave, forget The Wanderer
was lamenting lost heroes, The Seafarer grieving
for his lord and livelihood. I picture them, one close

to unmolested earth, the other on the whale's way,
and start to believe life was better then than in a world
with technologies deadlier than ancient monsters.

The new bird feeder rocking recalls me to today.
It's all rush, flutter, sending off and a stranger
with a dark stripe on its head, an aggressive beak

and a yellowish bloom on its breast that echoes
the dabs of sun which have appeared in the sky.
Suddenly I know this newcomer's a nuthatch,

feel gratitude and while I pour cereal, cut a piece
of bread, a clutch of words hatches in my head,
and a voice whispers: *this is as good as it gets*.

Oh Moon

multiple in shape and mood, I can't resist you
as slip of an eel with tips longing to touch
and kiss, as a silent circle of self queening
the measureless iris-blue that's only
an optical illusion, as an orange sun hung
low in the sky to herald cornucopia,
as Salome in swirling veils, a saviour who throws
light on dangerous passageways. Oh moon,
ferrier of calm to those enduring pain
in tousled beds, lean over the homeless
lying in sweaty tents, search out the terrified
who've fled to the mountains where they ward off
cold at night by huddling in crevices to sleep,
bring them your silvergold bracelets of hope.

Deer

Day or night they reappear from nowhere,
the to and fro of their distress an echo of mine
when panic rushes upon me and each time
I question, as I did then, how someone
who'd dreamt up gardens with mango trees,
myrtles and herbs from all over the world,
could believe captive deer would enhance
such an Eden. Their fleet movements belong
to the wilds of hills where they can run unseen,
their stillness to privacies in woods, their mystery
to forests dense with dark where any human
glimpsing a head bearing stately branches,
eyes which are softly-lit lamps, would sense
the animal innerness Artemis revered.
Yet there they were inside a wire enclosure,
huddled among spindly trunks with nowhere
to hide from children's squawks or prying adults,
jerking again and again into flight, shock
shrieking from eyes as they raced from end to end
of the world that caged them. That was years ago
but I can still feel the pulse of their terror.
And isn't this the fear which drives people who live
in places where each moment's weighty
with threat, to rip themselves from their homes,
risk their lives in frail boats and trudge
through dusty miles of languages whose jabber
they can't understand, clinging to the hope
of a life which won't cage them in dread.

Before Supper

Weighted with the day that's now darkening,
I climb upstairs, shed the dourness
with my shoes, coax life into a candle

and, unafraid violence will barge through
the window, I lie on my bed, watch
the flame licking up air. Needles of light

are fanning out from the core
into the unlit room, penetrating the cool
of the wall-mirror. A sudden ray

travels soundlessly up the duvet, glides
through the centre of my spread body
rivering it with reddish gold,

and the mirror announces the door
behind me is open. I'm surprised to see
the ceiling lampshade, which lures moths

to its deadly parchment, has gone
but the moon, a yellowish moon, is alive
on the landing. It seems to carry confidence,

this sphere whose circling preserves
our planet. For a while I forget the gunmen
who killed in the name of religion,

forget that race is attacking race
and the pain, sharp as pieces of glass
to bare feet, which so many endure.

Reluctantly, I blow out the candle,
give up the comfort of illusion,
go downstairs, switch on the cooker.

The Totem Stump

A loved landmark, taller than a man,
it stands as if on guard on a Roman road
where a path takes off between trees.

Hockney picked out this character, painted it
as a rugged torso in magenta and blue
with scar circles which could almost be eyes.

It holds out short benevolent arms, seems
to give audience to saplings on striped grasses
and people who travel from afar to pay homage.

*

Who came in the silent night with a chainsaw
and can of red paint, sweated to butcher it,
strewed the remains round the raw stump?

No way to resurrect the hefty trunk. Minor,
this piece of vandalism when violence
blooms every day but its slaughter haunts me.

*The Totem Stump which features in some of David Hockney's
Yorkshire paintings was destroyed one night in 2012.*

I Pegasus

lift my hooves for gallop,
rise as my white wings open.
Wind rushes into my pricked ears.
Excitement whinnies from my mouth,
ripples through my flanks, drives me
towards a place that's always cloudless.
Below me are snow-spattered peaks,
valleys where rivers wander, where trees
are laden with oranges, small suns
which pay homage to the sphere above.
Below me are huge cities with domes,
spires and innumerable buildings,
the tallest invade the blue of sky.
I miss nothing: the glassy stare
of cars stampeding like maddened cattle,
humans fleeing from burning towns,
forests felled like mighty armies,
the sea hurling itself in fury
at the land, barren fields thirsting
for water, skeletons of starved creatures.
I choose a verdant slope when I land,
hoof its milky grass and a spring
bubbles up from earth that's rich
with squirming worms. Then I rejoice
for I am the breath in and the breath out,
I am the quickening which comes unbidden
to the mind, blossoms into words
that tug the heart, I am sounds which bell
the air and enthral the ear, shapes
and colours which come together
to sing. I counter hatred, destruction.
I will not be stamped out.

Lifting the Sky

for Paul my qigong teacher

Plant yourself in the quiet on a familiar floor
or on an uncut summer lawn

and, thinking of seabirds, stretch out your arms,
let them ascend through the unresisting air.

With palms facing upwards, travel your hands
till your fingertips almost meet,

then release your breath, begin to separate yourself
from the weight of all that lies on you.

Allow your mind to open to this moment and your arms
to rise as they lift the palpable blue

high above the crown of your head.
Your wings will fold away

but raise them slowly to the blue again, maybe
a lightness like liquid amber will flow through you.

*Lifting the Sky: an exercise in qigong, the Chinese practice of
breathing, movement and meditation.*

Part Three

Edge

for Dilys

August 31st

I could weep, I've dreamt of Turner's Blue Rigi
for years and years but today the mountain
is misery grey, the lake surface steely
as repressed anger. I'd banked on doing sketches
of scarps, rocks and gullies to jump myself
out of the impasse I'm in.
                  Of course the kids
are spellbound – the train rising above
the trees is a mystery flight but these sparsely
grassed slopes are echoes of my bleakness. And now
mist has wiped the view.
                  We've stopped. 'Thomas,
must we alight in this freezing nothingness?'
'It looks like it, Mirie. I'd better carry
Rupe.'
        'I know you're big, Allie, but hold
my hand.' God, I'm terrified of slipping
into space...
            'Oh Thomas, look, an arrow!
It says: hotel – through this tunnel...' Unnerving
to grope in the dark. A word that's lit: *Press*.
Pray that a lift will hoist us up to safety.

17th September

It began on Rigi, that chilling platform,
the scary sense of standing on the planet's rim.
Then up on the snowy summit the drifting mist
rolled away and tiny cows were visible
on green pastures and miles below I glimpsed

67

the easy lake, its glinting, unending sapphire.
But the whiteness dropped again and I thought:
this is life: moments of illumination
which are snatched away. That was when it crashed
into my head: all you've achieved in yours
is one exhibition in a nowhere place,
the sale of two paintings. Why ever
did I believe I had talent? Suppose I'm scrabbling
to climb the unscalable and fall, fail?

21st September

A&E, its awful restlessness,
I've been trapped in here for hours, the doctor's
very poorly knifing me again and again,
and guilt screaming at me for being asleep
this morning.
        I wasted over half the night
on an abstract lakescape beyond saving
which meant Allie, white with fright, wakened me
yelling, 'Come to Rupe!' The child had a fever
so high he was hallucinating.
        Was it guilt
or what when I bundled him into the car
feeling my hands were useless, like butter slipping
from the wheel? I hope to god I'm in time.
        Thomas
was nearly voiceless with exhaustion last night
from days reporting that siege in Lincolnshire –
I mustn't phone him.
        'You ok, Mrs Lane?
Your boy's doing good, come and see him.'

23ʳᵈ September

Buckets I wept when I saw Rupe asleep.
He looked like a Fra Angelica angel.
Surinder – such a friend, taking charge
of Allie, feeding us both with scrambled eggs
and honey cakes which melted in the mouth.
Somehow she wrapped us in her serenity.
That was two days ago and now Rupe
is galloping round on the stick he calls *horse*
but I can't forget, can't forgive my failure.

24ᵗʰ September

'Mirie, how I wish you could wipe your parents –
their bloody expectations out of your mind,
they're not around. To qualify as human
you're not required to be a perfect mother,
cook and artist.'
                    'Painting's the point of my life.'
Oh god, I'd not meant to blurt my failure
tonight – he's really shattered. Why am I fetching
the crappy painting?
                    'I guess you're in transition –
you need freedom to work. An au pair
is the answer, you've been left enough money.'
He can't see a smidgen of talent. So why
nod instead of saying: what the hell for?

September 28th

*Our kitchen's wrong. Filthy smoke is gushing
from bonfire logs, flames are bullying the house.
Help! they want to attack the stairs, they'll reach
the children.*
                    I'll unearth the stairs. A tom-tom,

the beat's relentless in my head. It'll burst
if I don't uncover the stairs. Here they are,
behind the smell of coats.

               Oh no, they're trying
to push me down but I'll climb up. Allie,
you've become a pale snippet, keep away
from the smoke.

             I can't – but I must make my hands
quench the fire. Rupe, you've got to waken.
Wake up.

          Awake, in bed, swamped with guilt.

October 3rd

That poor tottery thing – her body's humped,
her face is a crumpled cabbage leaf. Why
does she care about the date her parcel will reach
Bangladesh?

          And what's the point of queueing
to post anything to anyone
or standing wedged between shelves of frippery
in a passageway of hell?

            All I can see
are the years ahead hanging like empty buckets
with nothing to put in them but grim routines
of home and school – it's all meaningless.

October 5th

Useless, Doctor Burns. Her meagre smile
was hateful. 'Mrs Lane, you've got children,
a good husband,' she snubbed when I said I felt
as if I was marooned on a grim riverbank
and everyone I knew was out of reach
on the other side. Then she dismissed me with pills.

October 7th

Face it, I've fallen over the precipice.
My hands become lumps of bloodless clay
if I try to paint and I panic. Matisse believed
he was going mad in Collioure but oh god,
he was alive, he painted – I'm just pretending.
Allie's sensed I'm askew. I'm failing Thomas,
we've not had sex for weeks, seem so separate.
Although he offers kindness he fails to see
I'm just a humpty, can't be put together.

*October 9*th

The plaque says: The Parlement of Fowls
and yet it's Victorian law courts – so pompous
the mock Gothic windows.
                              They're birds – the barrister,
the jury. The vulture judge with a gobble throat
is Doctor Burns. And now a cassowary
is hissing at me: did you abandon Allie
and Rupe?'
              'I won't answer a bird.' I'm blustering.
'Nothing will come of nothing, speak to the point.'
The judge, she's threatening me. 'I've never abandoned
my children.'
                'Don't try and bandy words.
You've shut them out of your heart.' She's hit the nail.
I love my children but my heart is nothing
if I'm not a person, can't paint.
                                    The judge
is rising now: 'Guilty of cardinal sin, chop
her hands.'

Flutterings of little red wings,
a mob of black feathers, beaks ready
to strike. Nowhere to hide…

It's scratched, my throat.
The softness of sheets. Thomas asleep, unknowing.

October 11th

They need time to kick in,' Thomas said
when I said the pills weren't working. I tried
explaining that shopping, making meals, collecting
the kids on time panics me and how words
in a book are blanks, dead. 'Worry,' he said.
'Have you found an au pair?' He looked so stressed
I lied I'd phoned round a few agencies.
Crazy, I've got to psych myself up
to tell him I can't bear the thought of a stranger
seeing me in fragments. Just before we ate
he hurled a can of beer on the floor and swore
but I was well aware it was me he wanted to crush.
My hands turned to stone – how did I dish
the measly meal? My friends try to coddle me:
'Mirie, it's standard stuff, depression hits
us all.' They don't see I'm beyond help
now my painting's dead. Only Surinder
suspects, tries to tell me it will pass. It won't.

October 12ᵗʰ

Houses collapsing like cards, an acrid smell,
Everyone running, a child screaming.

No escape.
My body's turned to granite. I must be armless,
look, my fingers are lying in the rubble.

72

October 13th

Repeating, I keep repeating Hopkins' words:
No worst, there is none. It's true and I'm full of shame
that the world's despair has tipped into mine,
blackened it. The frost that's eating its way
into our heatless house is gnawing me.

                                   Oh god,
the plumber breezing in. 'Good you called me,
a cold winter's ahead.'

                             I can't bear the smell
of drains he's wearing. If I don't support myself
against the kitchen wall I'll collapse. Winter!
I'm struggling to survive the next hour but how
to exist while *he* clumps around and cackles
about our leaks...

                        Now the ferrous stink
of that man has started to fade Hopkins'
O the mind, mind has mountains; cliffs of fall
keeps saying itself as if begging
to be painted.

                   Into the studio –
perylene black, the largest flat brush
and yes, zip a louring mountain, plaster it
with huge tumblings of rock...

                          Of course, it's fatuous,
a baby chimpanzee would do better
but it's sinister, belongs to the underworld
I'm trapped in.

                   Oh hell, it's twelve. The car keys,
they're not in my purse, my fingers all dither.
I'm late for little Rupe – losing it completely.

October 14th

Useless to sit on my bed and chew over
Allie opening the studio door

and accusing: 'You didn't paint a single thing
today when I was at school.'
                                        The kids won't stay
downstairs drawing for long. The Samaritans –
you mustn't duck phoning again…
                                        So caring,
the voice I'm blurting crap to about pieces,
despair. 'Sorry, I'm not making sense.'
'Yes, you are, I've been in that place myself
and I want to tell you there *is* a way out.'
Oh no – Allie.
                        'Mum, you've got to come
at once, Rupe has drowned my picture in his milk.'
Hold the screaming inside and snuff the call,
abandon hope, descend to chaos downstairs.

                                *

His face was grey as the grave as he let out
he expected he'd be in York a few days.
It forced me to drop the thin veil, weep
I couldn't cope and beg him to stay but he pinned me
against the wall and hissed: 'Don't be silly,
you know it's our income.' He doesn't seem to care
about my plight but he changed tack.
                                        'I know
you need support, I've phoned my mum. She's happy
to come and help.'
                        Happy! I escaped up here
before I yelled: not the knitter of jumpers
who can't tell a Renoir from a Rembrandt.
I've hit the bottom of hell now.
                                        If only
I could slip into a dreamless sleep tonight
and wake up feeling rested, believing
I can still find a life.
                        The knockout pills
that Thomas takes when he's away from home?

Yes, the bottle's lurking in his muddle. Four
should give me oblivion until tomorrow.

*

So deep in fluffiness and swampy warmth.
Pulling me up.
                    'Stop it, I want to stay
in feather-sleep.'
                        'Mirie, you must wake up
and drink lots of water.'
                              'You're hitting words
into my ears, Thomas, it hurts.'
                                      'Sorry.
I love you, Mirie, I won't be going to York
but we need to get you quickly to hospital,
you've taken – '
                    'Why, is Rupe at hospital,
Allie?'
          'No, the children are fine.'
                                  'Some people
are pushing me around. I'm dizzy, Thomas.
The stairs are shaking. Hold me, I'm going to break.'

October 15th

Oh god, my head – it's a steel bar. I'm injected,
punished.
              Unbearable, the lights yellowing,
swirling –
              mad as Van Gogh, his café lamps.
Put them out.
                  Oh stop the mouths, the stab
and stab of: 'Why' and 'how many did you take?'

October 17th

'I hate it here, Thomas, the people, their problems
make me ashamed of mine and sad for them
but they're pushing me down. A skinny girl,
a model, has nerve rashes and blisters crawl
up her legs like crabs, she can't bear her partner
touching her. A mum of triplets keeps making
cups of tea but spends the night screaming
and someone grasped my arm to tell me voices
invade his head and order him to eat forks
and babies' fingers.
                          I need to come home
and find a person to help me fit my pieces
together.'
            'Take a breath and leave a space
for me to speak, Mirie! They *want* to expel you
now they're convinced you didn't, thank god,
intend to die. I'm tracking down an au pair
to help you and don't start again that she'll run
the moment she sees the state you're in.'
                                    'But I'm drugged
to the hilt, my mind is scrambled eggs – '
                                          'The pills
are just for a few weeks to calm the storm!
You're still lovable.'
                  'Oh Thomas, hug me.'

October 19th

'A nightmare that prison, it's good to smell
the world again. Drive slowly, Thomas,
my head's tight as a kettle drum.
                              'I feel
like an edgy cat – your mother doesn't approve
of me.'
          'You're wrong, Mirie, to her you're gifted,

76

a star shining beyond her reach.'

'I'm a failure.'

'For Christ's sake, forget that rubbish! Listen,
helped or hindered by the kids, she's busy cooking
a special lunch with apple crumble. You're a queen,
they can't wait to welcome you back to your palace!'

October 21st

It won't leave me alone, Allie's painting –
the way she shoved the thing at me, its pattern
of violent red stars and circles black
as hell. Holes, she called them, her face sharp
with accusation. I've harmed her, it's unbearable
and so is everyone showering me with kindness.

October 23rd

Fishy fingers are burning. How to shift
the grill pan? Oh god, I'm fingerless,
can't paint a child in my crying book.
The kitchen's wriggling with fingers.

None are mine.

October 25th

Waterlodge, a canalside warehouse once
and now a school for problem people. I went
because they promised me a therapist.
The art and crafts space made me shudder,
there's no way I can help the other pupils.
Two are desperate to get off dope. I struggled
with yoga. Watching ducks squabbling for bread
and the nutty smell of autumn lightened things
walking home but here I'm nothing. Surinder's

77

helping with Rupe and Thomas shoulders the rest.
I'm dreading tomorrow when Yvette arrives.

November 1st

Even indoors the smell of leaves.
                              'You like,
I cook you boeuf bourguignon for supper?'
Her waif face is pretty when she smiles.
'It's your night off.'
                    'I like to be family.
My mother's man in Rouen is always cold
with me.'
            Poor girl – to think I was scared
of having an au pair here a week ago!
With her apple cheeks and dark hair, the chyrsanths
she picked in the garden – she's a Bonnard painting.

November 4th

What is this treeless place? A moonscape
beyond the cliffs of fall?
                        That's odd, a cupboard.
My butterfingers must open it for Allie
and Yvette.
                Only a bottle spilling seeds.
I'll plant them in soil on this little floor.
                                    'Mummee!
I've made you a cup of tea.' Yvette watched me.
'Oh Allie.'
        'You never take me to school!' My fault,
her anger. 'I will today.' She looks puzzled.

November 9th

'Oh great – I like artists who go for paintings
which revel in reds.'
                            'But I've stopped using
bright colours and I can't call myself
an artist now, I'm in pieces.'
                            Can't believe
this talk in a narrow room plastered with Matisse
and Hockney prints, prettified with knick-knacks
and cushions or Cassie in shorts and crumpled top,
the queen of this palace.
                            'Tell me more
about your painting.' 'For months nothing I've done
has a spark of life. Trying to cling to it
made me ill.'
                            'Did it? You've said you've failed
family and friends. Now you're sure you've failed
at painting, your passion. Suppose we've changed places.
Tell me would you suggest I carry on
crossing myself out or what?'
                            Oh god
she's flung me back to that gifted kid at school:
I'm not as good as a proper artist, Miss.
'No, I'd say: it's time to start trusting in – '
I'll choke.
                            'Try to be kinder to yourself
until we meet again. Have a peppermint.'

November 11th

It let something in, the session with Cassie.
I went off and studied a heap of pears
on a stall, people, our garden wilderness.
Allie opened the door and stared at my face
as if she knew and, oddly, Rupe barged
at me and uttered a whole sentence, his first.

79

Today I've been trying to puzzle out
why I became obsessed with landscape
in the abstract. Suppose I paint anything
which catches my eye – that crimson-hatted woman
dragging her dog past a tangerine van?

November 14th

'It felt as if the sun was emerging, Mirie
when you smiled at suppertime.'
                                        'Cutting down
on pills has unfogged my head but now I'm a page
that's blank.'
                'Didn't I see your sketchbook
in the hall?'
                'I've doodled notes but nothing's triggered
a genuine idea. You're worn to a frazzle,
Thomas.'
                'It's funless writing about abuse
in a miserable motel but I've good news:
mainly editing from Christmas.'
                                        'I'm really pleased,
I so wish I hadn't drained you, failed you, Thomas – '
'Stop it, I could beat myself for not seeing
the straits you were in. We're rising above the slough,
we're close again. Mirie, it's been so long,
I want to touch…'
                        'Oh god, I feel as sexy
as a block of wood. 'I don't know who I am
or – '
        'Sweetheart, I'm not a predator,
I want to help you. Suppose I stroke you gently,
my little rabbit?'
                        'Yes, stroke my shoulders,
they're like walls.' 'To me they're beautiful slopes
for fingers to slide down…'

So soft and pink
the blur of warmth and skin. 'Stroke my breasts,
kiss me everywhere, Thomas, I'm melting...'

November 18th

The art space I vowed I'd never enter.
I'm in it now, propelled by the image that's dogged me
all this week.
                    She's smiling, that English rose,
offering grainy paper and tubes of gouache –
it's so Rossetti, her sweep of dark hair,
her creamy cheeks.
                    Fingers trembling. Exciting,
the first spilling of paint onto paper,
sketching out the kitchen...Focus on the sill,
the chrysanths with fading petals...
                              Now, the kids,
I want their arms and legs in easy movement
and orange...Yvette with apples, yes, unfussy
as Dufy.
          To mix impression and detail like this
is a revelation and what I want now
is to rush away to the place where I belong
and work in my studio. Nothing to stop me.

November 19th

Alive again – a bit fragile but alive.
It feels good to be absorbing faces,
streets and lit windows defying night.
Was it to escape the self I didn't trust
that I turned away from painting peopled places
hoping I'd find fame? Success isn't fame.
I see now my real subject matter
is under my nose. I think the kitchen painting

might be going somewhere and I know I want
to teach again – I could use art to help
disturbed kids at school. A shock, Allie
grabbing the sketch I did at Waterlodge
and yelling at me not to change again
into another Mum or she'd tear it up
but I calmed her down and I'll build up her trust.

November 23rd

'Clearing the jungle garden is not special,
I won't, Mum.' 'But rides in the wheelbarrow
when you and Rupe have helped Yvette to sweep
the leaves and going out for fish and chips – '
'Oh yummy special.'
                                        Breathe in the damp earth,
the decay. Light is silvering spider threads,
roses are still madly in bloom.
                                        'Thomas,
I wish you'd cut this welter of brambles back.'
'Christ, the thorns will rip my hands, Miri!'
'Take my padded gloves.'
                                        We're hardly Monet's
Argenteuil, here – just a hint of it though
with trees and those sprawling bushes.
                                        I'd like
to do a sketch with figures by the wall and start
a series of paintings with doors open to rooms
mute with misery or singing out their colours,
rooms where hope is coming into blossom.

Acknowledgements

Credit is due to the following publications where some of these poems first appeared:
Acumen, Agenda, ARTEMIS, At Time's Edge – Remembering Anne Cluysenaar, Envoi, Frogmore Papers, Her Wings of Glass, Iota, The London Grip, Lunar Poetry, The North, Persephone in Finsbury Park, POEM, Quadrant, Scintilla, Stand and What Women Want.

I want to thank Erwin Schneider, my husband, for giving me both the space to write and practical help over many years. I am indebted to Dilys Wood for her belief in my work and invaluable feedback, particularly on the narrative poem, *Edge*. I am grateful to John Killick who was the publisher of my early collections and who looks at most of the poems I write, Caroline Price for detailed comments on problematic poems, Mimi Khalvati for her insightful feedback and the Sunday workshop group. I would also like to thank Les Murray who has published poems of mine in *Quadrant* over a long period of time. I am indebted to Stephen Stuart-Smith of Enitharmon Press for supporting and publishing my work for over twenty years, also Isabel Brittain and the rest of the dedicated team who work or have worked with him. Finally, I want to thank Katherine Gallagher for introducing me to the qigong class at Bounds Green and its excellent teacher Paul Flavell.

About the Author

Myra Schneider has lived in London since she was nineteen. Her first collection of poetry, *Fistful of Yellow Hope*, was published by Littlewood Press in 1984. Since then she has had nine full collections of poetry, mainly from Enitharmon Press. The most recent is *The Door to Colour* (2014). She has also had three pamphlets from Second Light Publications. Her other publications include fiction for young people and three books about personal writing. The two still in print are *Writing My Way Through Cancer* (Jessica Kingsley, 2003), a fleshed out diary with poem notes, poems and writing ideas; and a resource text written with John Killick, *Writing Your Self* (Continuum Books, 2009). She has tutored for the Poetry School since Mimi Khalvati started it in 1997. She is consultant to the Second Light Network for women poets and has co-edited five anthologies of poetry by contemporary women poets. She was shortlisted for a Forward Prize in 2007 and her work has been broadcast on Radio 4 in Poetry Please.